Y0-BXG-153

The Gentle Counsel of White Cloud

Larry G. Wayne

and

Grace P. Johnston

Editors

Detselig Enterprises Ltd.
Calgary, Alberta

© 1989 by

Larry G. Wayne and
Grace P. Johnston

Canadian Cataloguing in Publication Data

Wayne, Larry G.
 The gentle counsel of White Cloud

 ISBN 1-55059-005-7

 1. Spirit writings.   2. Spiritual life.
I. Johnston, Grace P.   II. White Cloud (Spirit).
III. Title.
BF639.W39 1989   158′.1   C89-091283-1

Detselig Enterprises Ltd.
P.O. Box G 399
Calgary, Alberta T3A 2G3

SAN 115-0324

Printed in Canada   ISBN 1-55059-005-7

To Grace
my gift from God

May peace flow through you,
happiness surround you, and love engulf you;
this is my gift to you.

To Shirley Anne Burroughs

in appreciation for her
loving support and inspiration.

For You: May your footsteps be blessed
as you travel along life's highways and byways,
allowing the joys and the happiness of the Divine
to radiate, to flow freely through you.

White Cloud, Teacher of Spirit Guides

This illustration of White Cloud is reproduced by permission from an original drawing by Coral Polge, renowned psychic artist of London, England.

Contents

Detselig Enterprises Ltd. appreciates the financial assistance for its 1989 publishing program from

Alberta Foundation for the Literary Arts
Canada Council
Department of Communications
Alberta Culture

Introduction

On the other side of death is a complex spirit world. There life continues in an unbroken stream, where we pick up where we have left off, our memories and personalities intact, our quirks and obsessions unaltered, our strengths firmly implanted, where we create our own heaven or hell, as we did on earth, according to the degree of our spiritual evolvement. The purpose of life is this very evolution, the inexorable movement back from whence we came, to the Creator, to Perfection.

The way is sometimes perilous, often serpentine, but always rewarding, if seen in truth, as part of the Divine Plan. Given the import of the journey, not surprisingly there are many who would help us, as service to others is a mark of spiritual riches. Selfless giving comes in many forms, but among the more remarkable is that offered by spirit guides.

Everyone has a spirit guide, sometimes called a doorkeeper or guardian angel. Before our birth, this spiritual helper covenants to watch over us, to inspire us, to nurture us, and to direct our moral growth. Whether or not the ministering moves us, enlightens us, or uplifts us, the guide must remain with us all our days.

The task of the guide is no simple undertaking. It requires much preparation, the patience of Job, and the wisdom of the ancients. Instilling worthy precepts into guides is every bit as crucial as relaying the message to mortals.

One of those elevated souls charged with the responsibility of teaching guides is White Cloud. He is part of the Great White Brotherhood which has nothing to do with race and everything to do with the spiritual forces of Purity, Truth and Service.

For years White Cloud spoke through the late Dr. Elsa Lund, the channel for the counsel of this book and the mentor of Larry Wayne and Grace Johnston. He speaks now through the latter two.

Addressed to a circle of listeners, the gentle counsel of White Cloud is for everyone. It rings like a daily devotional, revealing a disarming simplicity. It begins with broad guidelines, clear meridians with which to set and reset one's bearings. These meridians represent the finest ethical teachings of the masters – stand firm for the truth, walk the middle path, see the lessons in life's hardships, give so that you might receive, blend the spiritual with the material, live for today and not yesterday or tomorrow, and fashion your own paradise here and now.

And yet in White Cloud's hands these simple essences exhibit a remarkable, expansive quality. His blessings are like the loaves of bread and the fishes at Galilee, with their strange multiplying ability. They disclose more on each reading. They are pearls of wisdom which when beheld, when prayed about, build on themselves, yielding more understanding.

The most valuable single insight is not that there is a kindly motivated God, or that life is a constant struggle between light and darkness, or that beyond the great divide, existence is much as it is here – for countless others have said these things, and all will sooner or later know them. Rather this insight has to do with the power of thought itself.

Thoughts are not trivial synapses in a temporary brain, sealed off from the outside, from the universe, or the Great Divine Mind. They link individuals to the Creator. They are living things with great potential for good or evil; thoughts today are reality tomorrow. Whether or not a person has the slightest inkling that there is a God Power, a Force, or Energy that orders and suffuses all things and grants our wishes, thoughts, most fundamentally, are *prayers*. Within simple restrictions, they are granted automatically as the gift of the Great Spirit. They are the motive power of the Divine Plan. And no soul is excluded from the plan simply because he or she does not believe in it.

Providing the asking and the receiving are

within the Divine laws (and this heartening book is a first primer in those laws), there is nothing to fear, nothing insurmountable, nothing unattainable. White Cloud's soothing counsel is not another sad doctrine of the utter wretchedness of humanity, or the hopelessness of the human condition. In these short pages there is more honest hope, accessible hope, than in a mountain of murky manuscripts on philosophy in a bottomless bin. This hope is founded on the spark of divinity in everyone and on the judicious use of everyone's thought.

From White Cloud's guidance comes a secret of prayer – the knowing within. The knowing within is the God Power, for once faith is established, all things are possible. If we know within, the thought or the petition that is sent out is pure, uncompromised, unadulterated. We receive back, or manifest subsequently, the strongest thought we emit on any subject. If it is for material riches, upliftment, or the resolution of particular problems, so be it; if it is fear of ruin or loss of position or power, likewise. For here is the other side of this Divine arrangement. We choose, we petition; the Great Spirit provides. Granting free will, He does not separate our wise thoughts from the purblind, giving one and withholding the other. We may have what we want, though we must assess it and consider others before we ask. Ultimately, visualizing all the *finest* things or all the *worst* things that might happen is the precise way of *making* them happen.

Though there are many proofs of the existence of spirit for those who will accept them, and though this book is another evidence, its principal value is as an exercise in right thinking, in the importance of activating realizations.

The reader must not come disarmed of his critical faculties. If there is fraud or deceit here, the counsel must be rejected. If there is darkness or confusion, if there is vanity or conceit, ignorance or foolishness, if the advice smacks of evil or chicanery, cast it adrift. If it stirs the lower emotions of anger, lust, egotism, envy, or excess, discard it. If there is the slightest compulsion, leave it. If it does not work, release it. Submit it to the test.

And when the testing is done, in these assuring and upbearing pages will be found many messages of light and love, emanating a warmth, inspired, insistent, and unmistakeable.

David C. Jones

Invocation

Greetings, my children! Some of you know me by name, and for those that do not, I would reveal myself to you. My name is "White Cloud," and I have spoken to you on several occasions.

My children, I ask each and everyone who comes to this sitting to come with enthusiasm, knowing full well that we shall accomplish many things. My work is to teach upon the spirit side of life, and upon the material side of life. I teach others to help each and everyone of you so that they may guide you along the pathway. We, of the spirit, can but show you the doorway and we can open the door, but only you can walk through that threshold.

My children, greet each and every day with enthusiasm as each day is a beautiful day. Look at the beauty around you and in all things. Soon you will find the negative falling away from you, and you will see only the positive side of life.

Now, we will join together to accomplish what we desire, sharing together this short period of time and knowing full well that each one shall benefit in some manner. Look on it as a beautiful experience of learning, one step forward in the right direction on the pathway of life.

And now, my children, many blessings upon each and everyone.

1

Your Spiritual Spring Garden

Greetings, my children! It is a great privilege to be able to share this short time. I would like to speak to you for a little while about your spring garden. It is not too early to start on your spiritual spring garden.

Let us begin by clearing out all those negativities, doubts and fears which spring up into our minds at this time. Let us plant in our spring garden and in our consciousness, thoughts of all the ambitions and the desires we have ever held in our minds.

Let us plant them and allow them to grow sweetly and cheerfully, full of joy and enthusiasm. Let us bring on bloom and beauty for each and everyone here now. Let the winter winds blow away all those negative thoughts, clear the spring air so that we may bathe in the brilliant light, in that beauty and peace, and allow it to flow freely through us.

It is your right by and through the laws of God to have a beautiful garden in your hearts at this time. So, my children, do not neglect your spring spiritual garden. Take time to cleanse, and I assure you, each and everyone, you will feel that freedom – freedom from the bonds of fear and doubt and all negativities. Allow yourselves to shine brightly as the flowers shine in the sunshine. Feel the cool breeze gently around your hearts and your faces. Take time to clear your beautiful spring spiritual garden, and then you will know its joys.

Footstool of Learning

As we approach the footstool of learning, let us come in harmony, peace and understanding, sharing together the many things we are working towards, and may we progress in the manner we desire.

Please, Father, enter our hearts and show us the way to that peace and happiness, so that we may grow in understanding of the Divine Life Source and receive the many spiritual and material blessings of that Great Divine Energy around and about us always.

And now, my children, thank you for your love. I know you shall be successful in your efforts.

Begin Each Day with Joy and Happiness

Many blessings from that Great Divine Universal Brotherhood around us all. May we share together that harmony and love which is in each and everyone, and may we draw from that Divine Presence that harmony and joy that dwells in each one.

My children, sometimes we appear to be in harmony with the universe, with our brothers and sisters, and all is well, for we experience that complete harmony, love and understanding. But at other times we feel depressed and wonder from whence it came, and we say to one another, "Why is this happening, what has gone wrong, what did I do that I should not have done?"

My children, when this occurs there dwells within, negative thoughts and vibrations, which do not come upon one quickly, as they gather slowly like the storm clouds in your sky. You may say, "How can I get rid of these vibrations which are around me, which I do not understand, which I do not like and which I do not want within?" You must realize your error and draw quickly back on the path from where you have strayed.

You will find in all instances that you have strayed slowly from the path and allowed those storm clouds to gather. So when you arise each day just think to yourself – today is going to be a day of happiness and joy for me, I shall not see those storm clouds, they do not exist, I will put them from me and live within the Divine Laws.

My children, continue to do this each day, and when you retire to your bed in the evening, take a short time for meditation and meditate upon your day. Examine it and see what you have done that you could have done better, or what you can put right by changing your concepts on a particular idea or feeling, or whatever it may be, and then lay your head down to rest, knowing full well that when you awake there will be a new dawn. You will have a new day before you, and the sun will shine with happiness, joy and peace. Do this for the next while and you will see how much lighter your load will be!

Gifts of the Spirit

Let us draw from that peace and that Divine Love which surrounds us always. Dwell within it, live within it, and as you go forward, ever forward, you will grow within that Divine Love. And so, as you live your life in this peace and this harmony, guided by these ideals, so you will evolve within the spiritual realms.

My children, you will discover that you will

develop those gifts which are natural to you – your gifts of the spirit! Your eyes will be open to many things. You will be shown much by and through your intuition and your feelings. You will be guided at all times. Use these gifts for they are given to help and to guide you in your life. Accept them and know they are natural, for there is nothing difficult or unnatural about the gifts which your Divine Father has bestowed upon you. My children, live your life to the full and enjoy your life, for that is the will of the Divine Spirit.

And now, my dears, we shall join together with many others who also spend these moments united in harmony. Know that all things are possible within the Divine. Know that you have much power within you, and use it to the full.

Know Your Desires

Once again, we go forth together into that golden silence forgetting all things of the outside world. Let us draw close together in harmony and faith, knowing well that as we ask, so shall we receive. May we thank the Great Divine Spirit for the many blessings of happiness and joy which we have received in the past days, and may we fulfill that happiness and joy with enthusiasm.

Now, as we go forward, we all are doing what we have to do to fulfill the whole as a unit, working together in harmony, one for another. We know that as we cast aside our daily tasks and join together for a short time in that golden silence, we shall be fulfilled and receive our rewards.

There are, my children, many joys for you to experience if you will but allow the Divine to work through you. As you know, your heaven is here now. Enjoy all things that come to you now and remember, my children, there are many doors and many choices for you to take. Before you open any of those doors, know your desires, know what you want to fulfill those desires, know what is going to make you happy, and know that you can open any one of those doors at any time. If you will look within yourself, and look to the Divine, and know what you want before you open any doors, then you will know what is behind those doors. And the door of your choice will be good.

Remember this, my children, it will be good and it will be fulfilling. Do not attempt to open any door unless you know what you desire behind that door. Know that God or the Divine with His love is behind each door of your desire. Go forth in happiness and in joy, and know that my peace goes with you, my children.

Corners in Your Life

As sure as the sun rises with the dawn, so shall your pathways be revealed to you. As you walk that pathway you encounter a corner. As you travel along the roadway of life you will follow your path around that corner and all things will straighten out for you, and you will have gained a greater understanding by and through having turned a corner in your life.

My children, be not afraid of life, live your life, and if you do with the understanding and the love that God has for each and everyone of His children, so you will learn to live each moment as it comes along.

Do not live your life in fear of anything, and remember those corners in your pathway are but lessons of learning. They are not stumbling blocks, and you will learn much from them. My children, put your faith and trust in that Supreme Being who rules the universe, who is in control of all things. Know this and go forward and walk your pathway with a firm, steady step.

Live your life with love, and the understanding will come to you. Now, my children, bask in the sunshine and the love which is around you and enjoy it to the full. There is much for you to learn, and as you go forward, know full well that each day will bring forth a new dawning of understanding. Know this and do not look upon any problems or emotions that are negative. They are there for you to learn from, and I know you will do so.

Now, my children, I hope I have helped you in some way. Remember these things and use them and live them in your daily life. Do not cast them aside. Carry these thoughts in your heart, and all will be well with each and everyone. Remember, we do not come to chastise anyone. We come to help, knowing that if you will accept the help we strive to give, you will progress in your material life.

Learn from Yesterday

I ask each and everyone to come with me and relax, allowing that pure white light to shine forth and radiate through you. Feel the warmth and the love of that pure white Divine Light which flows within the Source, bathe in its beauty, relax, and give thanks to that Great White Spirit for the many blessings you receive from day to day in your lives.

I ask, my children, how many opportunities do you pass by? How many opportunities do you close your eyes to and not see? Remember, yesterday is gone; yesterday is something from which you can learn. The things of yesterday are your learning experiences. Today is an unfoldment; today is for progress. Go forward and learn from the experiences of yesterday, but do not dwell on them, only learn them well. Do not close your eyes, and do not walk as a blind man and miss your mistakes. Learn from them, but do not dwell on the past.

My children, go forward today and unfold as a flower into progression. Walk with a firm step and know that all will be well in your world. Accept all the joys that come your way and greet each day with enthusiasm. Observe your learning in the things you perceive, see your learning on the face of a child, seek your learning within all things that you experience, and you will progress far.

We Shall Reap and Receive in Kind

Once again we join in harmony, knowing full well we shall receive what we desire. As we send out our thoughts today, we shall reap and receive in kind.

Remember this, my children – in all things keep your thoughts on a higher vibration, as thoughts are carried out to others. Do not allow your thoughts to dwell and become negative.

You may talk about certain things that have happened which must be talked about, but when you do, make quite sure they are honest, positive vibrations, knowing that everything will be all right. You yourselves bring about the things you desire most in your hearts, and it is only by sending out thoughts in a positive manner that you can receive back thoughts on a good vibration from others you contact day by day. Continue sending out good thoughts throughout your lives in all situations, and you will be rewarded by and through your own thoughts.

I know it is difficult at times, but once you realize that you must lift yourself up to that Higher Force then all things will go in the right direction for you.

A Spiritual Prayer

Oh, Great White Spirit, we your children come together to go forward in harmony, in love and in peace. May each and everyone remove negative thoughts and resentments as we come before you. We stand at your footstool in the Divine Light, knowing full well that we walk hand in hand with you. We shall gain much and be prepared to receive nothing but the best, which we can only do by living now and forgetting all past resentments.

And now, Father, we place ourselves in your hands and in the hands of all those who are here to help and guide us. And we do thank you, Divine Father, for the great privilege of being able to come together this way.

2

Look to Your Mental and Spiritual Growth

Greetings, my children! I am so pleased that we are able to gather here again. My peace I bring to each and everyone, knowing that you are all children of God, children of that Great White Spirit which is around each and everyone, and is a spark within each and everyone.

My children, always remember that you are part of the whole, and you may at any time demand what you desire, what is going to make you happy. It is there for you to take. It is there for your asking. What you ask for, you will receive.

Look to your mental and spiritual growth day by day. Visualize it as a lovely garden filled with many beautiful flowers, trees, plants and green, green grass wonderfully groomed. You must understand, my children, that your garden must be nurtured and cared for, it must be watered and groomed, and the sun must

21

shine down upon it.

Also, my dear children, please remember that in your beautiful garden weeds sometimes grow which must be uprooted and taken away. You cannot have a beautiful garden with a growth of weeds. The weeds in your beautiful garden represent the negative thoughts that surround you day by day, and they must be weeded out so that your spiritual garden will grow with beauty and strength. By doing this and allowing none of the negative elements to exist, only the beauty shall come forth and your garden will grow with the brilliant light, the beautiful rays of the sun and the gentle breezes. It will grow in love and peace and understanding at all times.

So I say to you, my children, look at your garden and see what has grown within. Take stock of it and look after it so you may enjoy all of God's creations that come your way day by day.

There are many blessings if we would but look for them. We are so busy looking for things that do not concern us. We are so busy concerning ourselves with others that we forget to take stock and look after ourselves. Our first concern to God is for each and everyone to realize and say, "I AM." God in His great wisdom will take care of all of His children, one by one, in His own time and in His own way.

So, my children, go forth and allow the sun to shine in your garden and enjoy all the wonderful things that are there. And now, I leave you with my blessings and the blessings of many other brothers and sisters who are around you, and may each and everyone shine within that Divine Love.

Power of the Mind

I would like to say a few words taken from somewhere else: "Blessed are the ties that bind our hearts in holy love; the fellowship of kindred minds is like a holy love. . . ."

My children, I would like to speak to you on the power of the mind, lest you forget the Source of the power which all minds draw from. Use that Source as it is there for you to draw upon. Many people utilize this power. Some use it wrongly, or apparently wrongly, inasmuch as they appear to get their own way, and we may say, "Oh my, that person has done this or is able to do that, why?" The reason, of course, is that he too is drawing from the Source and using it for his benefit.

So, my children, why don't you use that Source for your own advancement! As you know, it is there for you to accept, and all things are within that Divine Mind or Energy, or whatever you care to call it. All you have to do is to open up that flow and allow that force to guide you. Ask for guidance. Do not thoughtlessly use this power. Think and consider what you desire and what is going to do you the most good. As you know, the way to do this is to visualize what you want, what you desire. Put it into motion and then forget about it. It is so easy. All God's laws are free from constraint; they are not difficult.

So, remember that Source is there for your use. If you do not use it, that is your fault for not putting it into action. You can have anything you desire by and through the use and power of your mind. Your mind is a mind of all; within the mind is everything you ever wanted, as you too, my children, can draw from the Source.

Just remember, there are many ways you can draw from the Source. You can ask for guidance and then you must stop and listen for that guidance; whether it be from your brothers and sisters, or whether you draw directly from the Source, it does not matter. But use that power, my children, for it is something you have neglected to do. You have forgotten one of God's laws; it is there for your use.

Now let us put ourselves into the hands of that Divine Spirit and use the Divine Mind for our experiences in our gathering. By putting it into action, we know we shall receive results, good results, and you will be surprised at how quickly and effectively our sittings shall progress.

Remember, my children, use this power for your own benefit and realize that whatever you put into the Source, whatever you allow to flow, so you will receive unto yourselves. If you put into the Source greed, anger and envy, that is what you will receive in return. So, my children, again, just think and consider what you desire and what is going to do you the most good.

Now my dears, I leave you with my blessings knowing full well we are going to receive that wonderful flow, that wonderful knowledge from the Source that is going to put into effect what we desire.

Walk the Path Lightly

Walk the path lightly knowing surely that as the darkness comes, so must the daylight shine forth again. If you would but walk in the sunshine and realize that the negatives only tend to bring you worry and frustration. . . .

Follow the bright path of sunshine and know that all things will be brought to you. Do not allow negative thoughts to show themselves to you at any time. Replace them with positive thoughts, and you will find that your life will be much brighter and much happier.

There is no need to travel that pathway of darkness and frustration. Lift up your thoughts and look towards that brightness, and know that with your own thoughts you will bring to yourself upliftment, joy and happiness.

Walk within the Divine at all times, hand in hand at the footstool of grace and understanding.

Radiate Divine Love

Let us always radiate the Divine Love, for if we would but dwell within that understanding then there is nothing we would fear, there is nothing to fear.

Remember, my children, put the past behind you. The past is gone, it matters not. Look not to the future, it is yet to come. Live your life now and allow the Divine Intelligence to guide you. You are well blessed, my children, each and everyone of you. You are well loved, my children, each and everyone of you – remember this! Go forward and do not allow those fears and anxieties to rear their heads so that they are uppermost in your minds. Get rid of all those anxieties, worries and frustrations. Cast them from you and know that from now on you are going to live your life in joy and happiness, and so in this manner you will receive much help from those who love you and who are best able to help you in your daily lives.

And now, my children, many blessings. Look forward, never backward and be happy. If you are happy then we are happy – know this!

Drink Freely of the Waters of Life

May that Divine Essence fill your environment with love so that we all may radiate love, one to another. May we each walk in that Divine Light which surrounds us and shines so brightly that we can not help but feel the presence and the power of that Great Source.

May we, each and everyone, drink freely of the waters of pure life. If we do, we will never again thirst. So go forth, my children, and drink freely of the waters of life. Drink and your life will never again be negative, as you will always live in the light.

Use this advice, use it freely and use it with authority, and when you speak, speak with authority and mean what you say. Allow the words to flow from the Divine Mind by and through the help of your spiritual brothers and sisters, and always speak in truth.

All of you digress at times because you are afraid; you fear what another will think; you fear you are hurting someone else.

My children, do not be afraid. Speak always in truth. But remember when you speak in truth, it too can be a two-edged sword. When you speak, speak without pride and not for other reasons, such as satisfying your ego or someone else's. Just be yourself and speak in truth. By doing this, you will be drinking freely of the waters of life.

Put Your Trust in God

Put your faith and trust in that Divine Intelligence, allow the knowledge around you to flow, and allow yourself to draw from that Divine Intelligence.

We have gathered together many people at this time to share within our sitting, harmonizing one with another. I ask each and everyone just to relax, open your minds and allow that essence from the Divine to flow through.

And now, my children, we have work to do both on your side and ours. Put your trust in God and know all will be well. We are working one with another for the good of each, and if you will but put complete trust in the Divine, it will give you courage to carry on your days on your earth plane.

Help from Spirit Guides

Once again it is a great privilege to meet, and I thank each and everyone for the joy and the happiness that you bring to our hearts by and through your presence and your loyalty in these sittings – together, one with another, sharing with all your brothers and sisters, creating great peace and harmony in your lives.

Learn to draw from that Divine Source, that Divine Intelligence which is open to each of you, and by Divine Intelligence I am speaking of the higher brothers and sisters who have greater knowledge than we have. If you will just open your mind in acceptance of that Divine Power, then I assure you that you will be surprised at what you will receive, which will help you both materially and spiritually in your daily lives.

Remember, my children, there is nothing wrong with asking for assistance from any of your brothers and sisters, as they are always ready and willing to help you in any direction with guidance, upliftment and encouragement.

It is within each other that we find this completeness, this oneness, we are seeking.

To Bless is to Receive

Why don't you do this for the next period –

bless each and every situation which arises in your material life? If you do, you cannot possibly harbour negative thoughts or ideas from yourself or anyone else. If you truly "bless" all situations as they come before you, you can find only love, joy and happiness in them. I know if you do so, your life will change considerably.

How can you yourself be unhappy or miserable whilst you are blessing? To bless is to receive, and you will receive many things as a result. Experience this truth as you go along, and you will know and understand far more than you do now.

When you "bless," remember to do it from the heart and mean it with enthusiasm. I speak of situations which arise within your daily life from time to time, which can and do bring about and draw to you all those negative vibrations.

A Spiritual Prayer

Oh, Great Divine Father, your strength is our strength. As we go along the highway of life, may we reach out our hand to you and draw from your Infinite strength, knowing full well that it is always there for us to lean upon and that it is given freely to each and everyone.

And now, my children, fear not as there is nothing to fear within your life. Bring to fulfillment this realization and put your faith and your trust in that Great Divine Spirit, and all will be well.

Many blessings upon each and everyone.

3
Schoolhouse of Learning

Greetings, my children! Once again it is a great privilege to share with you this time. May each and everyone join together in harmony and understanding. May your lights shine forth so that all may see and recognize the brightness and the love which radiates.

My children, do not falter and do not allow your footsteps to drag along the pathway. Walk firmly, put your feet down and walk strongly within the faith of your heart, knowing that as you do, all will be well. It is when you falter on that path that you lose faith in yourself and cause yourself to be hurt and to have problems in your heart, which should never be.

Remember this, my children, stand firm for what you believe is right, for what you know is true. Others must follow their pathways, and this you cannot change. All you are concerned about is your own walk in life, which in time to come will be your own spiritual walk in our world.

This pathway you are travelling now is a schoolhouse of learning, whereby you will benefit when you come to our side of life. My children, learn well your lessons, as they are there for you to see. If you do, you will make your pathway much easier than if you fight and struggle along the way. So, my children, hold your heads up high, and know that in the end you are the ones who are going to benefit, and you are the ones who will make much progress in your material world. You are all learning your lessons and as you progress through kindergarten to high school and through other studies, you will learn them well.

And now, my children, the time has come for us to progress further.

Walk the Middle Path

My dears, as you walk hand in hand towards the radiant sunshine, there is much for you to do in your life on this material plane.

As you live your life here, live it to the best of your ability. Enjoy it and fulfill it now. Life upon your earth plane is a two-edged sword. At all times, you must walk within that middle path, never any extremes of any kind.

Always stay within that pathway, for if you do not, you will walk upon quicksand, and you will find yourself in trouble once again. Walk in the pathway of light. Balance your life with the spiritual and the material, blend them together, and you will not get into any trouble.

My children, we are always by your side to guide, uplift, encourage and help you at all times as you embark on what you must do. And as you fulfill these desires in your life, so you are helping us to make our progress, as we in turn are helping you to make your progress, and so it is balanced.

My children, walk that middle path at all times and do not step over into the quicksand. Always be aware of what you are doing and know full well that everything will be fulfilled with the Divine. All have their work to do, and it will be done. There are many joys to share, and I say, send out that joy within your environment for all to share and allow that radiant happiness in you to shine brightly.

And now, my children, I leave you with my blessings, and my peace goes with you always. Thank you for your patience and understanding. I shall help you with the work ahead.

Count Your Blessings

Let us go forward into the light, casting from us all shadows, casting away all doubts and fears.

As we join together in harmony, allow that Divine Spark of love within our hearts to shine forth. I ask each and everyone, how many times throughout this material day have you counted your blessings? Even though the weather may be stormy at times, there are still blessings to be counted. I thank the Great White Spirit for the many blessings I have received this day, and I thank you, my children, for your kind thoughts, for your love and for the blessings you have given me.

So, my children, do not look for the storm clouds, look for your blessings day by day. Acknowledge them, accept them, and know they are there for all.

Oneness with the Universe

Let us at this time visualize a long ladder which we are about to climb to the top. Step by step we go along into the brilliant light, that white light, and as we reach the top we will stay in that white light. Visualize and feel the warmth therein, and feel the peace, that great peace within each and everyone.

And now, in that wonderful peace, we radiate and feel that Divine Presence; our souls and our minds are in harmony with the universe. Feel this oneness with the universe and all in it. Within the roar of thunder and the flashes of lightning, we see that Divine Presence. Within the sands of the desert, in every grain of sand upon the floor of the desert, we see it.

Now, we bring forward our awareness, our spiritual awareness and our material awareness, and we blend them together so they may harmonize as one. Feel this and know it is so, at one, in harmony together. And now my children, you have learned much. Use this knowledge knowing fully it is within the Divine Plan.

Now, I must ask you to step down from the ladder to a halfway point where you will remain in the warmth and comfort of the light.

Greet Each Day with Enthusiasm

Let us go forth together into the brightness, into the brilliant light and leave those outside influences, and let us strive to understand why we are here and what we are doing, sharing together one with another.

My children, as I have said before, let us not dwell in the past for in the past dwell our mistakes and our fears. Let us take from the past only what is going to help us now. How can we receive the many blessings here for us day by day, if we dwell on negative thoughts of the past and the future? This, my children, we cannot do.

You look into the future and see things which are not there, which do not exist yet. Why do you persist in allowing those thoughts to come before you? Put them out of your mind, and accept the beautiful blessings around you now. Allow those blessings to flow to you!

You can only do this by and through a positive attitude day by day. My children, as you greet each day, greet it with enthusiasm and know it is going to be a beautiful day for you. See only the beauty in your day and live from day to day, not from week to week or from year to year, because many of the concepts you have now for tomorrow may be wrong.

Just live for now and allow your progress to come to you by and through the love of that Divine Father, who is there to shower His love and His blessings upon each and everyone. Do not walk in fear, for there is nothing to fear.

Just live for your happiness and enjoyment, being ready to receive on a spiritual level, and you will make your progress on that spiritual level always. Do not allow yourself to be brought down by the negative thoughts of others. Cast them from you.

Just look at your life and realize how many negative thoughts you have been open to receive from others. You do not need to do this if you will just live from day to day and look for God's blessings as they come before you.

Remember, my dears, God's table is laden with good and bountiful things for all.

Lift up Your Thoughts

May the Great White Spirit be with you and walk with you always. My children, walk in the pathway of the Great Spirit; do not walk in the shadows. Watch your thoughts and your feelings at all times.

Remember these words, "Cast your bread upon the waters and it shall return to you." That great teacher did not mean for you to throw your bread upon the waters to feed the fish in the sea. The meaning is clear and simple. As you send out your thoughts, so they will return to you; as you perform your deeds, so shall they be returned to you.

Always remember, my children, to count your blessings each and every day. You would be surprised at the great love and the many kind thoughts that have been directed your way. With your appreciation of these things, so will you receive and gather more and more unto yourself.

You, my children, have travelled far, and you still have a long journey. I mean a spiritual journey to your heavenly Father. You will be called upon by and through the presence of many around you to help others, and by helping others, you will be helping yourself and all who are helping you.

Patience and Preparation

Remember, my children, there are many paths to take and many ways to reach the peak. Go your way and walk your path, knowing full well you will eventually reach the end of the road and dwell within the Divine Spirit.

My children, I know you are going forward as there are many things ahead for you both spiritually and materially. Take full advantage of each and every opportunity that is brought to you along the way, knowing surely that as you travel along the pathway of life there will be many to guide you, to encourage you, and to uplift you.

Now, my dears, remember in the way of God no great or good work is ever accomplished without patient preparation.

You also have Your Part

As we gather together, there are many whom you do not know now who are helping and guiding you in your tasks. You also have your part to do, inasmuch as you send out love and harmony to keep the vibrations high. Thus we shall accomplish much together.

You yourself have progressed far, much further than you ever imagined possible. There are still many steps along the pathway to take, and I know you will be guided in the right direction by and through your own brothers and sisters who are ever close. Listen to the advice they give and earnestly work upon it. Accept and know that the Great White Spirit, whom you call God, will never let you down. Put your faith and trust in that Great Divine and go forward.

And now I will leave you. We have much work to do, and it gives me great pleasure to come and speak to you in this manner. I know you listen well and that makes my journey worthwhile.

My children, I know you will always walk in the light, and you will never turn your back upon your learning or upon your brothers and sisters. This I know, as I have trust and faith in you, as you have in me.

When Nothing Happens

When no phenomena occur one is apt to think and wonder, "Am I wasting my time? I have been sitting for a while and I do not seem to be making too much headway in my spiritual progress."

Remember my children, many feel this way

when sitting for development, and many fall by the wayside because they are impatient. Spiritual growth requires patience and faith so that the spirit may unfold.

My children, you are never alone, you are never left to fight difficulties of this material world by yourself. Unseen, often unheard and sometimes unfelt, the influences of the spirit world are always round and about you. Remember, your guides are not angels of darkness, seeking to lead you to paths of confusion.

My children, your guides are close to you, just as close as your thoughts. Thoughts travel fast, as does telepathy. Your guides are close even when it seems they are unheard and unfelt. They come to you because they love you, and the love they have for you makes them desire to serve you and work through you.

The truth they teach is the truth of the Great White Spirit, that knows no limitations. It is for all not for one; it seeks to take everyone in its loving embrace.

My children, may you become aware of that great power ever around and about you, the great love, the inspiration that seeks to express itself through you, and the truth that is waiting to be revealed to you.

So, my children, work within the laws at all times so that you may become better instruments for your guides to work through.

A Spiritual Prayer

Oh, Great Divine Father, we are gathered here to accept the embrace of your love and understanding, which we would share one with another, and may that great love encircle us now and forever.

May we come to the realization and understanding of that great love, to know what it really means to us as individuals and as part of the group.

We know that as a group we can go forward and do what you would have us accomplish, but we can only fulfill this by and through that full knowledge and understanding which we are slowly gaining together. We do thank you for allowing us to come together in communion, one with another, for a short time, in order that we may all gain knowledge, one from another, so that we may grow in our awareness and understanding.

Oh, Great White Spirit, we, your children, place ourselves in your loving care, your loving hands, to help and to guide us through the tides, over the mountain peaks and through the raging storms, which we know, if we would but realize, do not exist at all.

4

A Spiritual Meadow

Greetings, my children! Once again we come together to share this short time. I ask each one to visualize a beautiful, brilliant and warm light, a shaft of light which you are going to feel that will lift you up into brightness and tranquillity.

My children, as you go along you will feel a cooling, gentle breeze around and about you. Stepping now from that radiant white light onto the soft green grass of a peaceful meadow, you sit down with all your brothers and sisters who are gathered around you.

Now, my children, this is where you will receive much inspiration, and whilst I have the opportunity, I say to each and everyone, enjoy the things that are brought within your life, enjoy the things in life you wish to enjoy, and you will find your happiness and happiness in all things.

And now, my children, enjoy your spiritual meadow with all your brothers and sisters. My blessings to each and everyone.

Face Up to Your Problems

Once again we come together to share the joy and the love of that Great Divine Intelligence, the Divine Spirit that works in and through the great universe, being in control of all things, at all times, and that functions by and through the nature of all things.

My children, remember that God or the Supreme Intelligence is all loving, all knowing. He knows your needs and your requirements. You have only to ask in faith and in love, and you shall receive these things. It is the knowing within that brings all things about for each and everyone.

Let us remember that you yourself build up your obstructions which bring about many difficulties for you, and when you build these obstructions and are faced with your problems of life, you allow your thoughts to race in many negative ways. Face up to your problems once they have accumulated, but remember also, do not allow them to manifest. You can do this by and through the guidance of that Divine Spirit. Live your life in His guidance, allow that Great White Spirit to take you by the hand and lead you along the path.

You have had this happen to you many

times. Do not allow those obstructions to manifest. Put them behind you and do not permit your thoughts to race and accumulate in a negative manner. Live your life, be happy and enjoy the many things here for you to enjoy. Use all these things but do not abuse them, because by and through abuse you build up your obstructions. Understand what I am saying. I am speaking not to one person but to each and everyone and many who dwell within the spiritual spheres on the lower planes of thought. I speak to many people.

And now, my children, strive to live your life well. Steer your ships to a safe harbour at all times and walk that broad path. Walk in the light of that pathway, and all will be well with you.

You have each one made much progress, and I am well pleased with my children. I know that you have helped yourselves in many ways, and it would be of no use for people such as me who come to speak to you, if you did not use what is given to you.

Learn from Your Experiences

I would like to thank you for the opportunity to come and speak to you in this manner. To me, it is one of my many blessings.

Yes, my children, we receive our blessings

even on our side of life, and we experience and share many things with you. One blessing I wish to thank you for is the love that you send to me at all times. It is indeed a blessing to me to share in your joy and happiness which you experience from day to day.

And yet, my children, it is a blessing to share your sorrows also because within those sorrows comes learning and experiences which you benefit from, or should benefit from. Sometimes we do not recognize these as blessings but they bring about greater awareness to us, and it is up to each one to learn from these as they come along and not to fall back into the same pattern.

My children, learn from your experiences and your sorrows as they are brought about, so that you may become more aware of the things around you. Sometimes we do not learn from past experiences as we should, so these things are brought about to us. So remember this, my children, and know they are brought about for your own benefit because they are learning experiences. And remember that fear of any kind will drain your vital force.

Sometimes, my dear children, we do not even recognize our fears, and we allow a drain of that life force which is a Divine Force within us. When this happens we leave ourselves open for whatever comes along. Sometimes our fears are such that we are afraid we are hurting someone else, so as you can see, fear can hurt you in many ways. My children, open your eyes so that you may realize these things and learn from them, as this is why you experience them, so you may learn from them and not go back and do the same things over and over.

My children, that great teacher once said, "God is the light of the world, I am the light." The word "light" is mentioned many times and in its true essence is very valid. You, my children, are part of that light. You are the light of the world, also. So never allow that light to grow dim or to darken. Always keep that light shining brightly within and about you so that everyone around you may recognize your progression and know you have that something special in your heart.

Allow your light to shine in truth and love and understanding, and know that you are an authority in these things. My children, never falter and never allow anyone to drain away your vital life force, which is of God.

The Secret of Awareness

Let us go forth together into that sunshine, that glory, that peace which passes all understanding. Allow your inner being to dwell in that peace, remain there and allow nothing to disturb that serenity. Put yourself within that Great Divine Spirit and dwell there.

My children, within that Divine Essence you can come to your path. The glory of God will shine around and about you always. Put your faith and trust in the right direction, knowing full well that you will never be let down in any way.

My children, we draw close together so that we may harmonize one with another and uplift ourselves to that higher existence and dwell therein. We know there are many people around us to help us gain that fuller understanding of life within the spheres so that we may go forward one with another in harmony and blessing.

My children, remember to bless every situation that comes into your life. Do this and all will be well in your sphere, and remember also that you are only a light to the degree of your awareness, your awareness of what is going on around and about you. Use this awareness and be aware of all things both large and small. For it is only by being aware that you can come within the realms. Be aware of the breath of the wind upon your face, sense the refreshing coolness of a summer rain, behold the beauty of nature with her fragrant flowers and stately trees, feel the morning sun beaming brightly around and about you. If you do this every day you will discover the secret of awareness, which is to be aware of all things within your earthly environment.

As you become more aware of everything that is happening around you, so you will make progress within the sphere of your existence. Once you become fully aware of all things inside your sphere, then you will become aware of things outside it, on a higher plane.

So, my children master this sphere and you will have mastered all spheres.

Untangle Your Thoughts

Let us untangle our thoughts as we walk in the presence of that Divine Intelligence. I ask you all, as you untangle your thoughts and arrrive at your decisions, why do you not stand by those decisions?

As you have been told, your first impressions are always correct. I have seen many of you in this past period make a decision and then change that decision many times like a bird in a tree flitting from branch to branch, getting nowhere. How can we of the spirit help you, if we cannot keep up with your thoughts? When you make a decision, stand by it, whether it be right or wrong, for in this way you will learn something from it.

So, my friends, untangle your thoughts and

allow that Divine Intelligence to guide you. Put your thoughts in order, and know that you have made the right decision.

Speak in Truth

From harmony comes happiness, and with that happiness we rid ourselves of all fears and negativities, for one does not go without the other.

Grasp your happiness and keep it at all times. Do not criticize yourself or others disparagingly and do not criticize each other within the group. With your criticism, there is destructive criticism and there is constructive criticism, and only you within yourself know which is right and which is wrong. My children, understand this distinction. Speak your mind clearly and honestly at all times, and know that you can have complete harmony and happiness one with another.

Strive for that harmony and happiness and you will have made a great step forward. You all are progressing in many areas. I only offer you advice which you may choose to use within your daily life.

I say to each and everyone: Live your life fully and be happy.

Divine Light

Let us travel the broad highway into the Divine Light and through that Divine Light cleanse our hearts and minds of fears and doubts.

Visualize yourself within that Divine Light going forward into that Divine Consciousness. Feel it radiate around and about you, relaxing and comforting. Feel that contentment in your hearts and the joy of sharing together that brillance and purity there for each and everyone. You do not have to search for God. He is right here beside you and within you.

The Universal Law

I ask you to remember and to think very carefully of the truth that one only receives what one gives in life. One cannot expect to receive anything unless he is prepared to give something of himself to others. Remember this, my children, it is a law of the universe, a law of God's, the Divine Law.

"As you sow, so shall you reap." You give out joy and laughter; you shall receive joy and laughter in your life. You can think upon these things and recall the thoughts you have given out and realize what you will receive. This I know for truth!

My children, just think upon these few words and strive to gain a greater understanding. And now, let us go forward joining together to give of ourselves, knowing full well we shall receive, and let us give thanks for the receiving. It is the Divine Flow, flowing through each and everyone; as you allow the Divine Love to flow through you, so you will reach a greater understanding of all things.

Give Freely of Yourself

Each and every step that is taken along the Divine Path is guided by and through that Divine Power which flows to each and everyone.

Let us give thanks for the knowledge of that Divine Power, and go forward and drink of that knowledge; drink freely so that you will come to that great understanding. I remind you of a saying – "It is better to give than to receive" – and the meaning of this proverb is, that by giving you are receiving much, and by giving of yourself you are opening that flow of energy, the flow of good, the flow of God, which you are drawing to yourself even at this moment.

Allow that flow to come towards you, accept it and realize that in giving from the heart, you are receiving from the heart of the Divine which can become a continuous flow of satisfaction and benefit to yourself. So, my dear brothers and sisters, always remember to give freely of yourselves and you will receive much. It is a law of the Divine – *You cannot give without receiving, you cannot receive without giving* – and that is what life is all about.

And now, my dears, let us place ourselves in the hands of the Divine and allow that spirit to flow freely towards each and everyone in order that we may give freely of our own individuality.

Live One Day at a Time

May we walk within the laws of that Divine Force, and strive to live one day at a time. Do not look ahead, for you know not what is there. Today is now and tomorrow is yet to come. So, my children, I ask you to live within the law, just one day at a time. Accept all things within that day and enjoy the things that are brought before you. As a great teacher once said, "My table is laden, laden with joy and happiness." Accept these things, my children, and know they are there for everyone.

A Spiritual Prayer

Oh, Great Divine Father, may we all sit at your table and partake of the great joys and the many blessings which are ours to be had, for they are there within our grasp, if we would just come to the realization and know.

Oh, Great Divine Spirit, we would put our thoughts within your thoughts and draw thereby from the highest, the Divine Source, from which all knowledge is available to us. We place ourselves in your hands now, knowing surely that we are well taken care of.

5

Whenever You have a Problem

Greetings, my children! I say to each and everyone, whenever you have a problem, change the concept of that problem completely. If you would but change the concept just as strongly as you put out the thought in the other direction, then you would have no problems at all.

The strongest thought that you send out is the thought which is going to return to you. If you send out a thought in a certain direction and think of that thought strongly enough, so it will be. These things you have heard many times, but until you come to the full realization you will not have full understanding.

It is now time for you to have that understanding. You have many times received thoughts from other sources that were undesirable to you, but what did you do? You returned those thoughts in a negative way. Just change your concepts and send out in a positive way and know that what you do and say is right. If you do, there is nothing that can hurt you in any way. Come to the full understanding and the knowing, and all will be well.

If you would only give as much energy to do things the right way as you give to do them the wrong way, things would be different. You can cancel out negative thoughts sent to you by having strong positive thoughts yourself. Let us look at what we have learned, knowledge we have gained together. Let us use that knowledge to the best of our ability, use it with enthusiasm, knowing full well we will gain more understanding by utilizing the knowledge we already have.

I would like to speak for a few moments now on the problems of life which face each and everyone. When you have a problem, take that one problem, examine it, and use the knowledge you have acquired to solve it. And solve one at a time. Many go along the pathway trying to clear up all their problems at once. This you cannot do. If you try to clear up many of your problems simultaneously, your emotions get out of control and cause you more problems.

My children, take one pathway at a time and one problem at a time. By doing this, you will find that you will accomplish much more in the end. Do not rush out trying to clean your house all at once. You would not do this with your material home, you could not do it, and you cannot do it with your spiritual home.

So, my dears, take one step at a time and one problem at a time. You will find that you will clear up far more than if you rushed off in all directions. By and through this understanding you will gain much knowledge and a greater sense of the laws of God or the Divine.

My children, you will learn much more as you travel your pathways. So put your hand in the hand of God and walk in peace and truth. Go along steadfastly in the knowledge that all things can be accomplished at all times within the Divine. Know this, my children, and you will have taken a great step forward, a great step into that Divine Knowledge which is yours to have.

There are many ways to change those negative thoughts to positive thoughts so that your life can be much happier, more joyous and loving. Within your life, one way is to *bless*. To *bless* is to radiate joy, love and happiness. Why don't you all *bless* every situation which arises in your material life?

My children, if you truly *bless* all situations as they come before you, you cannot possibly harbour negative thoughts or ideas from yourself or from others. You will find only love, joy and happiness from all things. I know if you will do this your life will change considerably. How can you yourself be unhappy or miserable whilst you are blessing negative situations in your life? To *bless* is to receive; you will receive many things if only you will do this.

Experience all these things as you go along, and you will know and understand far more than now. When you *bless*, remember to do it from the heart and mean it with enthusiasm. I am speaking now of situations which arise in your daily life from time to time that can, and do, bring about and draw to you all those negative vibrations.

Walk in Truth

Go forward into that brilliant sunshine and never allow your footsteps to falter along the way. Never allow yourself to be dragged down into the darkness.

My children, you have learned much along the pathway, and you know enough now to keep that harmony, one with another, and never permit that harmony to be dragged into the darkness.

Keep your heads up high speaking the truth at all times. Walk in truth. If you do, then harmony and love will follow, and your footsteps will never falter. Remember, you are children of the Divine Light. That spark is in you; use it always and keep it alight in your heart.

Be a Shining Example

Let your light so shine before men that they shall see the good works you do. It is only by a shining example that you may help others along the pathway. They see and observe the fashion in which you walk the pathway, and as you set your example, so they themselves will ask and desire to follow the same pathway.

My dears, there are many laws for you to know and understand. One of these laws is that you cannot cast your pearls of wisdom before swine. You must be ready to accept the pathway to God, to the Divine, and no one can walk another's pathway for him.

My children, remember this always, for if you do not observe the rules of the Divine, how can you help anyone else? First of all, you must put your own house in order.

Now, my children, let us give thanks to that Great White Spirit for allowing us to gather here together in the presence of those whom you know as guides and helpers. Give thanks to all your brothers and sisters for they are ready and willing to help you along the way.

Harmony

Once again we come together in communion with souls from the highest sphere to harmonize together.

Remember, my children, that harmony comes only through understanding of one with another. Strive to understand your brother and your sister, know that they are walking their pathway which is right for them at this time, and know that eventually they themselves will come to a fuller, richer understanding of themselves and others around them.

It is only by understanding every situation in your lives that you can grow spiritually. Once you realize that many people put on two faces, then you can understand that there are many sides to their natures. One face they will show to you and another they keep deep within themselves. This is what I mean when I say, understand your brother or sister and then you will understand all sides to their natures and the lives they live.

Deep within everyone is a child of God, and deep within is that spark of understanding, but each one must grow in understanding to allow that spark to shine forth brilliantly through all those negative thoughts and wrong concepts that are around us. Each one must remove all false faces he shows to another in order that he may further understand himself and that group around him.

The Thoughts You have Today
You will Reap Tomorrow

Remember, my children, you cannot share anything unless you are willing to give. As you give, so shall you receive. We, on our side of life, share together our responsibilities. We know and expect that you, my children, will share together on your side of life your responsibilities, even within your gathering here.

As you give, so shall you receive, this you all know. The thoughts you have today you will reap tomorrow, whether they are good or bad, whether they are sharing or not sharing. You shall receive in like manner that which you give. Give to all your brothers and sisters, share with them the responsibilities of your circle here at this time. Just think of the work and the effort they themselves put into their endeavors with you and the time they spend sharing. I would like you to think on this in the next period. I know and you know that "as you sow, so shall you reap." You cannot give without receiving, you cannot receive without giving, and that is what life is all about both on your side and on our side. We also have to share with our brothers and sisters.

Whatever you put into your lives, you shall take out in like measure. Remember this, my children, and whatever you do for another never goes unrewarded, as it is always returned in some way to you.

Walk in Peace and Understanding

We ask, Oh, Great Divine Spirit, that you place a blessing upon each and every child here at this time. May they receive what they desire in their hearts.

We know that as we ask, so we shall receive, and so we place ourselves entirely in your hands, knowing full well the blessings are there for us to receive at any time if we would but recognize it, and they are there for our asking.

We do thank you, Oh, Great Divine Spirit, for allowing us to gather together for this short time. As we return to our homes, we shall each feel better for having been in your presence. We shall feel that upliftment, we shall receive the healing from those around us who, with joy and happiness and love in their hearts, are only too willing to impart from the Divine Source. All have their place within the Divine Cause, and all must do their part to make up the whole. If this were not so, there would be no purpose.

So, go forward, my children, do what you

have to do. Do it with joy and happiness in your hearts, knowing well you are doing what you must do. You can, and will, each one, do your part, as no one else can do it for you, and neither can you do it for others, as they also must fulfill what they have to accomplish.

Now, my children, I would like to address something on your minds. How often have you heard the one-sided conversation wherein one person does all the talking? To harmonize together there must be a sender and a receiver, otherwise no one would listen. I have seen this only too often – one person talking and the other sitting and listening. But neither one is listening. How much fuller becomes the Dynamic Creative Force when you go with your problems into the presence of God and you ask for help or guidance! You ask, but you do not listen long enough. You receive something, but then you start to jump up and down and wander off in all directions trying to solve particular problems. My children, when you ask, know you will receive the answer and wait until you get it before you walk in all directions. As I have said before, when you do this you only create more problems for yourself. So do take your little problems to that Great Divine Mind and sit in the silence and think, and you will receive your answer. Then you can put it into motion.

Many times you fall by the wayside, and

many times we must pick you up again. As you raise yourselves up, so you make more progress and grow stronger within the Divine Source. So, my children, walk your path. Do not walk the path for others. Walk your own path in the way you know you should. Now I hope I have been able to help you just a little.

Do What Makes You Happy

When things look dark to you, look towards your concept of the particular thing bothering you, and change that concept. Sometimes we have in our moments of darkness wrong concepts which to us appear right. But, my children, take another look at those concepts you have and change them so you may lighten your load.

When something is troubling us, we tend to look at things in a very different light from what we would do otherwise. So my advice, my children, is to look at the concepts. Remember to do the right thing which is to be happy. Only do what will make you happy. I know it is very difficult, and sometimes we fall by the wayside, but I am here to help you and to pick you up again.

So, when you think to yourself, "No, I cannot do that, it is not right," change your concept and say to yourself, "Will that make me happy?" No one else, just yourself. If you have any doubts in your mind at all, then reject it. Do not fear for anyone else, and do not fear for yourself.

My children, I promise you that if from this moment you will only do what will make you happy, then your life will be different. Each and everyone can do this, and I know you can take this realization into every area of your life and apply it. If you do, you will have no fears, because you will know that you are doing the right thing for yourself.

Just look at the people around you. They are doing the things to make them happy, not to please you, and in their way they are living their lives to the full. So, why can you not do the same? I have heard you say many times that people are happy doing their own thing. You do yours, and when you have done so, do not worry about it, no matter what it is. If you do this, then you will find that you are being honest to yourself. You are being truthful to yourself, and by being truthful and honest to yourself you will be happy within yourself.

Carry this out in every degree in your life. Consider no one else because all are so busy doing what makes them happy, even though they are miserable doing it. It does not matter, as you have progressed far enough now to know that it is essential to be happy and content in your life on your earth plane today.

If you can learn to be happy here now, then you can be happy in all dimensions, but you must first learn to be it within yourself.

Do Not Carry Your Problems to Tomorrow

Lift your hearts and minds to that Great Divine Loving Spirit that is ever close around us, that Great White Brotherhood that binds us each together, one with another, in mind and spirit so that we may join together in harmony, knowing full well that nothing can harm us.

As we draw ever closer to that Great Divine, we do thank you, Father, for allowing us to come together in this manner, and may we be eternally grateful for a loving presence around each and everyone, and for the presence within us all of that Great Divine Spirit.

My children, as you lift up your thoughts, close your mind to all things outside so that you may cleanse your spiritual homes within which you dwell, and then live each day moment by moment as it comes along. Remember also that any problems which arise in that time should be cleared out then. Do not carry your problems to tomorrow.

Now, my children, you are going upon another path, a path on which you will have much help as there is much to do. I know you have many brothers and sisters who are willing to assist, although you are not aware of the Great White Brotherhood which is around you and which will also share with you many hours of learning that you in turn will share with others.

My children, as you travel along the pathway, you will find that you will gather to yourself much learning and much understanding. Then, as you grow in understanding and love, sharing one with another, so your spirit shall rise and shine, shine forth for the glory which you yourself do not realize at this time. But you will, and you will live in harmony where nothing can hurt you. And there will be no sorrow because as those problems come along, you will solve them at the time they arise, so they will not be problems at all.

A Spiritual Prayer

Many blessings to each and everyone. May we share the joys and happiness together as we walk along the pathway of life, learning the laws of the Great Divine.

We ask Father that you would enter our hearts and show us the way to that peace and happiness which is beyond all understanding.

May we receive a great blessing and a great upliftment in having joined together in this manner to look upon the smiling faces of our brothers and sisters, walking together in truth and harmony.

6

Do Not
Be Discouraged

Greetings, my children! I thank you for your love and loyalty in these sittings. Remember, my children, your brothers and sisters and I are all travelling the pathway in the same direction. We are all, each and everyone, going forward as one together.

My children, it is only by falling by the wayside that you can learn your lessons. Do not forget that your brothers and sisters on our side of life are progressing in a parallel direction. We are not perfect, no more than you are perfect. How could we be? We as well have lessons to learn.

My children, you at times create many problems for yourselves which cause you to stumble along the pathway. Remember, do not criticize one another. Rather, stretch out your hand to your brother or sister who needs that help along the wayside. Do not be discouraged, for all of you have made much progress, and we on our side of life are very happy to see this progress made by and through the help you have received from all your brothers and sisters. You have put in much effort to achieve this progress. So, my children, never be discouraged and never criticize another. Go forward both materially and spiritually in a blending and harmonizing of both our worlds.

Each Stumbling Block is a Blessing

Let us go forth hand in hand into that brightness. It is shining around each and everyone. May we, as we go along life's pathway, remember to count our blessings. They are many. Even though we may stumble, we must look upon each stumbling block as a blessing which will bring us closer to that Great Divine Spirit. Let us give thanks every day for those blessings. Sometimes we do not look for the blessings which cross our path, we do not recognize them, and so we shut them out of our lives as we travel along the road. But remember, the love and the light of that Great Divine Spirit cannot be shut out of your hearts. Once you have started on the path so you must travel that pathway. And so my children, enjoy your path as you go along in your life day by day.

Enjoy the harmony and the love, for it is there for you to share together. Share that love with all your brothers and sisters, and they will reach out and share their love with you. Remember also, my children, that inharmonious thoughts only bring to you more inharmonious thoughts. As you give out, so you must receive. If you send out harmonious thoughts you will receive harmonious thoughts. Live your lives in complete harmony within yourselves and be happy. When you are in harmony with yourself you cannot be in disharmony with anyone else.

Each One Must Evolve Along the Path

Again we come together in harmony to seek the light that shines forth with all its brilliance upon us. Allow that light to warm your thoughts, bathe in the beauty of that brilliant pure white light which is around and about us at this time.

Remember, my children, there are many, many beautiful souls around you who are adding their light to your light, helping with the harmony and sending forth their love to each and everyone. Feel that love which surrounds you at all times.

My dear children, sometimes it seems there are people around you in your material life who appear not to be evolving spiritually in any way. But you must remember that those people are unfolding in their own particular fashion.

Sometimes the path is rough and thorny and they get hurt in many ways through their ignorance of the laws of God, the Supreme Being or the Divine Source, but eventually they will also come to some understanding as they evolve along the path.

When you come within the auras of these people, remember to lift up your thoughts and do not allow the negative thoughts, feelings or vibrations to penetrate at all. Remember, you have much love surrounding you and how could you possibly come to any harm by these vibrations, unless you allow it. So cast out those thoughts and vibrations which surround you, in the knowledge that one day those emanating them will evolve to a greater understanding at their own pace.

And now, my children, I do thank you for the love you have for me and the understanding, and the love you have for the Shining Ones around you.

The Two-Edged Sword

As you know, you may have anything you desire within the cosmos, and you have been told how you can accomplish those desires.

My children, this is a two-edged sword, and I would like to explain the danger. You can concentrate and ask for what you desire, whether it be happiness or knowledge, or whatever. But when you sit and concentrate day after day asking the cosmos to bring what you desire, you are falling into a trap, a dangerous trap.

By doing this you are worshipping false idols. You begin to worship what you want and this you will never receive, for you cannot worship false gods.

The correct way to attain what you request is to ASK and then KNOW you shall receive. Leave it to the Divine Source to bring your desire about, for the Divine Source knows how it will best be accomplished and perhaps it is not the way you would expect.

The Great Divine is Within

Allow your spirits to grow. Do not fetter yourself with doubts or fears. Know that the Great Divine is within each and everyone. Allow that spirit to manifest through you, and as you grow, so will your understanding grow. You will have no fears of the future. You will know that all things are within the whole, and you will not have to look for that two-edged sword, because with that greater understanding there will be none. You will walk in the light ever, casting away such things as anger, fear, pain, and you will not allow the ego to shine brightly.

You will have such things as understanding, peace, harmony and love – love for one another, love for each brother and sister, love that you have never experienced before. Your brothers and sisters extend this love to you always. It is there for you to reach out and grasp always. This great love surrounds you with the purity and the brilliance beyond your vision at this time. My children, go forward and know that all things will come your way.

Knowing Within

May we walk together into the light and allow that brightness to shine through each and everyone. Feel the warmth and radiance of that pure white light completely surround and uplift you. Allow yourself to dwell within the beauty and harmony of that light.

My children, the Divine is ever with you; that Great White Spirit of the universe is always there to guide you, know this! You can have whatever you desire, you can take your problems to that Great Divine Spirit and receive a solution to all your troubles. Know it and dwell within that Divine Power.

It is that *knowing within* which is the God Power in each and everyone. Ask and you shall receive. If you do not ask, how can you receive? Think on this and ponder it well. My children, we of the spirit are well pleased with your progress. You have endeavored to make progress, and through that endeavor it has been granted to you.

Now go forward and have no fear of the future, and know full well that there is much in God's course for you. Know that you will achieve your goals without any hindrances from anywhere. You will not be allowed to fall back into troubled waters. Go forward now into the bright sunshine, enjoy that sunshine, enjoy God's world as it has been made for you, and accept all opportunities as they come your way. Accept all things that are given to you, enjoy all the gifts of God made for your happiness, knowing that they come from the universe, because, my children, by refusing to allow others to help us or do something for us, we do not allow their lights to shine.

It is by and through each one that others who come before us are allowed to progress. We help them in many ways. You help them in many ways, and they must also make their own progress, and there are many paths to progression. So remember, my children, do not dim anyone else's light and always allow yours to shine brightly so there will be no dark corners and no dark clouds in your life.

How Great is Your Faith

My children, I ask, how great is your faith in that Divine Spark? Belief and faith are not the same. You may say, "I believe there is a power greater than ours." But I ask, how great is your faith in that power? My children, which is deeper – your faith in us or your belief in us, your faith in the Great Divine or your belief in the Great Divine?

Remember, my children, you are each within that Divine Power, and you can accomplish all things once your faith has been established. All things will come to you both material and spiritual. Use your faith to remove all negative thoughts from your life, and know that your faith dwells within the Great Divine Force. Once you do so, you will build up and manifest that wonderful faith within yourself which is all important.

You are Never Alone

Once again we come together to share our experiences, sometimes of the rain and the storms. But remember, my children, you walk through those storms and you come out into the sunshine once again. Just as the flowers and grass which grow after the rain, so you will grow. You will grow in strength and be able to stand firm on your own feet. You will have a greater understanding of yourself and others, knowing that you have gained much knowledge through your travels and experiences. Under those storm clouds you will travel through the vales and come out refreshed.

Be happy in the knowledge and the understanding that you have gained. And now, my children, join together in love, harmony and peace in the knowledge that whatever you experience is shared with others who guide your footsteps along the way.

Dwell Within the Divine Power

As we come together within that Divine Presence, feel the peace and the warmth which flows around each and everyone. Allow that inspiration to flow freely so that you may walk with the Divine, hand in hand, knowing full well that you can draw on that Source, that great Source of all knowledge which is available to all of you now.

May your footsteps be blessed as you travel along life's highways and byways, allowing the joys and the happiness of the Divine to radiate, to flow freely through each and everyone. It is there for you to use, especially at this time. Each one of you has walked the pathway of life. You have all had your ups and downs. You have travelled the rough waters, and now you are aware of the problems which face you.

I speak of the problems around you person-ally, which can be overcome very easily. They are not really problems; it is only the way you see them. If you would only examine those around you who frighten you, or who cause you worry, fear and anxiety. Do they care? No! Just look closely at their attitude towards life. They can take things or leave them; they are very sure of what they are doing.

And now, my children, how much more strength do you possess, each and everyone! All you have to do is know, know that your thoughts are much stronger, and know that you can use this Divine Power which you gain from the highest side of life.

It is the knowing and the enthusiasm in your efforts that bring about the desired end. Know that all your thoughts are positive thoughts, and being positive, they will always be the strongest thoughts. Your thoughts are not filled with vengeance or revenge because these thoughts would only be returned to you. You must realize and fully understand that no one can hurt you in any way. The only way is if you allow it.

Remember, my children, use your thoughts and your knowledge with enthusiasm and retain that *"knowing within"* yourselves. It is so simple. We are busy filling our minds with fears and anxieties of what someone else may be doing to us, and thereby we strengthen their thoughts and draw to ourselves more fears and more unnecessary frustrations. So, my children, allow that Divine Knowledge to flow through you. Know that there are many blessings ahead for you, and know that you have peace within your hearts always, if you so desire.

A Spiritual Prayer

My children, we come together in harmony, and we know once we have gained that complete harmony together, one with another, then we shall find complete happiness.

May we feel the warmth of the sun and the glow and the radiance. May it shine forth light in our hearts day by day.

May the blessings of the Great Spirit be upon each and everyone. May we have great joy in our hearts in the time to come.

May we walk in the pathway of Divine Love and Light.

7

The Pure in Heart

Greetings my children! At this time I would like to take one of the teachings of that great master, Jesus of Nazareth, who reached the "Christ Sphere." It is this: "Blessed are the pure in heart for they shall see God."

If we ponder for a few moments those words, we will see their true meaning. The pure in heart are those who walk in truth, love, harmony and understanding. If we possess these qualities, we know God. There are many who know these things, but do not use them or fully understand them. Many do not put these realizations into practice, which is worse than not knowing at all, because they have no excuse for not progressing.

And yet, in this wonderful teaching and its application is God, who is within all things. If you could only see it – within every blade of grass, and there are many blades of grass upon your earth plane, within every beautiful flower, and within every note of music. If you could just feel it, then you would know God.

My children, realize that consciousness within all things, and then you will have that understanding which will draw you close to the Great Divine Power, that Great Love. Each of you can have all these realizations: God is in the wind that blows, in the waters of the seas, in every grain of sand – have you thought of that? God is in every grain of sand, every blade of grass, every tree that grows, every bird that sings and in each and everyone of you. Realize this, my children, and you will come far.

The Higher Side of Life

May we dwell within that Brotherhood, that Great White Brotherhood, in order that we may draw from the knowledge therein which is available to us.

We are now aware of the things around us on our own particular sphere, you on your material plane and others in their own spheres. Reach out for that awareness, know it fully and use it to the fullest extent.

Now, my children, extend that awareness further; extend it into the higher realms, into a spiritual level. You will need patience with this one, my children, you will need to work hard to come to that realization of that awareness.

If you could but reach out to those higher

levels you would lift up yourselves, your minds and your spirits to that higher level whereby nothing would disturb you. You would then be aware on a spiritual level of all things. That is your goal. Now, go forward and know that you can attain it. Remember there are many people on our side of life, people who are within that Great White Brotherhood, from whom you can gather much knowledge, and they are ready to impart much knowledge to you as they work within the Great White Spheres.

Once you can lift up to a higher vibration then you will be able to tune into these brothers who are only too eager and willing to help you in all phases of your learning. So now, my children, as you have been aware of things on your sphere of existence, be aware now of things of a spiritual nature which are open to you, knowing full well you can be aware of all these things by and through Divine Association with your brothers and sisters of the Great White Brotherhood.

Go forward with enthusiasm and with gratitude to those who have gone on before for the help that will be given to you. As one of the great masters said, "Ask and it shall be given unto you."

Footstool of the Divine

Remember, my children, there are many from our side who are eager and enthusiastic, ready to do their work. I ask you all to share your enthusiasm and your eagerness, match yours with others' so you may go forward together. Now let us go hand in hand to the footstool of the Divine and open our hearts and minds to that great love which flows to everyone.

My children, that Great Infinite Love which is always overflowing is there for you to have, and now I ask each and everyone to joyously join all who are within our gathering, and we shall achieve much.

Stand Fast, Stand Firm

Oh, Great White Spirit, we ask now that you would shine around each and everyone. Let us receive that Divine Light direct from the Source, so that we may receive the many blessings you have for us, and may we give thanks for the blessings we have received. How many of you, my children, have given thanks today to that Great Divine Father for the many blessings He has brought your way? Oh, Great Divine Spirit, may we follow in your footsteps and come to your footstool.

My children, I say to you, why do you fear? You all have many fears in your hearts. Examine them and throw them out. Do not allow the negative thoughts to enter in, and you will be surprised with the happiness and joy that will come your way.

My children, I promise you now that those thoughts you fear do not exist. You are afraid of your neighbors and you are afraid of people around you! I say to you, no one can hurt you, go forward and know that you are walking within the Divine Plan.

Stand fast and stand firm, and know you walk in truth at all times. You walk the Divine Path, you walk in the Divine Spheres, you cannot do anything else.

Never Fear in Any Way

Put your faith and trust in that Great Divine Essence, that Being whom you call God, which is the essence of all things. You can receive only good if you will but place your faith in the right direction from where it originally came.

I know that each of you place your feet firmly upon a solid foundation and progress forward into that Great Power from which you have much yet to learn and understand. My children, as you go along your pathway of life, I know that each one is proceeding forward, and we of the spirit are very pleased to come along from time to time to help and guide you, knowing certainly that the end of the road will be a great benefit to all.

We do thank you for the progress you have made by your own efforts. We know you will paddle along your stream of life instead of blundering through the waves and the wind as you have done in the past. I am speaking now of past lives you have had. You have come to the realization, and all will be well. Never doubt the progress you are making, and never fear in any way.

And now, my children, go your way, go in peace, go in love and understanding. Have no fear of the future, for all things are being put together in their rightful order for each and everyone. We know that all have their work to do in your sphere and our sphere, and we shall work together hand in hand, in harmony, love and loyalty.

Put Your Spiritual Life in Order

I would like to speak to you about communion with those who are ready and waiting to help us in our endeavors. We offer our thanks to each and everyone, both on your side and our side, for the work they do.

Let us go forward into the light and drink of the waters that refresh and cleanse us. And may we offer our thanks to that Great Divine Spirit for the love and knowledge that is imparted to us by our reaching out to the Source.

How many of you have put your spiritual homes in order? It is only by and through living the laws that you have been taught that you may put your spiritual homes in order. It is of no use if you do not apply these laws. Once you have mastered all of them as you know them, then, my children, your material life will fall into place without any effort on your part.

The Great White Spirit

Let us just relax our minds and allow that Divine Intelligence to flow freely so that we may be within the beauty and serenity of that pure white light.

My children, as we go forward, walking along the sandy shore, we can feel the soft, gentle waters around our feet, with cool breezes that take away all the negativity of the day. Allow that flow of pure white light to continue around and about you, so that you may go to the top of the highest mountain to enjoy all the beauty that may be there for you to see. Stand there for a moment and absorb all that is within your vision; completely relax, filled with joy, happiness and enthusiasm.

Allow that enthusiasm to flow through you so that you may carry this exhilaration into our little gathering and enjoy all the beauty around you.

And now, my children, we shall return to our gathering here amongst our friends, our brothers and sisters, to share with them the great love and enthusiasm which that Great Divine Mind has bestowed upon us.

Remember, my children, the power of the Great White Spirit is there within your grasp at all times. Go forward with joy, love and enthusiasm in your heart.

True Happiness

My children, we have many times spoken on happiness, and I ask you to evaluate what happiness means to you. Does it mean riches, fame and possessions in any degree? No, it does not exist in these things.

We now progress deeper into our philosophy of happiness, for we have only begun to teach an understanding of this concept. Until we come to realize that true happiness does not exist in our material things, and unless we have that Divine Spark in our thoughts and deeds, we cannot in any way find true peace and happiness.

My children, truthfully assess your happiness and your values. Seek the Divine Spark in your happiness, search your soul well. If you do, you will indeed find great happiness in all things, for nothing is without God or that Divine Source.

All things are within that Divine Source, but we as children searching for enlightenment must seek that Divine Spark within all things. Start with your happiness and what it means to you.

Garden of Peace

I would like now to take you on a spiritual walk, and to begin our journey, I ask you to visualize a beautiful meadow.

Now, my children, simply step into this environment with ease, look upon the many beautiful trees and flowers of radiant colors, colors you have never seen before. Now smell the fragrance of those flowers and feel the soft green grass underfoot with the warmth of the sunshine upon your face.

Absorb the beauty and loveliness of this spiritual garden, and as we walk along you will see your many spirit friends whom you know and who know you! Stop for a moment and say hello; and now you will see the spiritual children, happily playing in the waters of a peaceful stream which gently flows through our garden.

Each and everyone is radiating harmony, peace and enthusiasm, and as your spirit friends look upon your faces, your faces also radiate these qualities. This, my children, is my garden of peace.

You too can have a garden of peace in your life. You all create your own Heaven or your own Hell depending upon which course you take. Do not worry about being happy, do not worry as to whether you are living the laws of God, for whilst you are worrying you are not being happy and you are not living the laws of God.

My children, I say to you, just *be*. And now the time has come for you to return to your surroundings, knowing full well that you have many around you who are waiting to work with you with enthusiasm.

The Broad Pathway of Light

Let us go forward and walk upon that broad pathway of light, those beautiful, powerful rays of pure white light which surround each and everyone. Within that light is perfection. Just as you are perfection in the centre, deep in your hearts, you must now realize, having that perfection, you can accomplish success in all things.

Remember, my children, should you walk on troubled pathways you may come for tranquillity and walk in my garden of peace any time. In that garden you shall rest, knowing that no one else can enter then.

Now I do thank all for their kind thoughts, their love and their devotion. We know that within the perfection of the light around us we shall accomplish much and have the success we desire in any direction we choose.

The Supreme Test

Once you have that Divine Spark in your heart, it will never leave you. My children, you have passed many strenuous tests that have been put before you, and I myself thank you for allowing me to help with your progression. All your brothers and sisters are very pleased and very happy. It is difficult to apply the laws when you are going through troubled waters, and that, my children, is where the supreme test is.

To you, my child, do not fear, as all will be well. You have gained great strength, and as you travel those waters you will gain greater strength. And to you, my child, I am very grateful also as you have shown great progress, and all your brothers and sisters are pleased, as you have followed the inspiration and guidance given to you. And to the medium, she herself knows the infinite love we have for her.

A Spiritual Prayer

Oh, Great White Spirit, we ask that our brothers and sisters on both planes of existence be brought closer together in love and harmony. May we be truly thankful for all the blessings around us, and may we realize those many blessings. I do thank you, Father, for the guidance you have given to each one on both sides of life.

May we truly walk in your Divine Love and Understanding, one with another in closer harmony, knowing surely that many blessings are available to each and everyone.

8

The Star of Life

Greetings, my children! Once again we gather together to share many things. If we could but share your Christmas spirit at all times throughout our lives – the joy and happiness that comes to many at this particular season, both young and old. If we would but cradle ourselves as children within that Infinite Love and wisdom and understanding of that Divine, the Spark, that reaches each and everyone. If we would but follow that star of life to reach our goals, as we go on so would we find a brighter star to follow to higher goals and a higher life. May we always reach for those goals we can hold forever.

Now, my children, there is much for each to do here on your earth plane. Reach that understanding of your fellow man and woman, understand everything on your material world – the birds, the trees, the wind that blows, the spark of God within your brother and sister.

Strive to reach that understanding, and do

not condemn yourself for past mistakes. I have heard you do this. Remember those past mistakes are sign posts in your lives to help you along the path and to bring you to a better understanding of yourselves. Do not criticize yourself! Do not condemn yourself! Look forward at all times! Your mistakes are in the past! Create harmony and you will have no disharmony. Live in harmony, and disharmony will disappear from your lives.

And now, my children, I do thank you all for your love and your kind thoughts which shine forth like beautiful stars.

Your First Duty is to Yourself

My children, grasp all the happiness you can conceive of. I have told you this many times. Take that happiness, but do not hurt anyone else whilst you do. My children, you have progressed, and you now realize that when I speak of happiness I am speaking in a spiritual sense also. Remember all God's laws are two-edged: you may take your happiness but not at the expense of anyone else, and this applies to all things in your life. It applies to everything around you.

Look for that two-edged sword, not the concepts you have had to the present. Sometimes people hurt themselves and you and others accept the blame for their hurts, but this is wrong.

So, my children, you must be aware of these things if you wish to progress at all. You cannot accept the responsibility for another person's mistakes. You can only accept the mistakes you make yourself, and once you have accepted those mistakes and realize them, then it is up to you to put them right. You have the knowledge to do this, and so, my children, we have gone one step further in your quest for understanding.

You must remember that your first duty is to yourself. You are the most important one in the eyes of God, or the Divine Father. He is only concerned with your welfare, yet as a two-edged sword, speaks with His concern for all His disciples.

The Wheel of Life

Let your brightness shine, let your light mingle with our light so that we may shine together, and we know if you do you will cast out all doubts and fears from your mind.

My children, walk in the light, walk in the light always, and do not dwell in those dark shadows in the corners of your hearts and minds. Do not allow them to come close, and if you will but walk in that light combined with ours, there is much brightness.

Remember that fear is a negative force just as strong as positive thought. If you allow that force to rule you, how can you walk in the light? Now, my children, remember these words – "Walk in truth and walk in light." If you walk in the light, then you walk within the positive. The negative brings about many things which are troublesome – fear, frustration and anger.

And now, my children, there are many blessings placed upon your heads. You have your little niche within the wheel of life which is forever turning and which you will realize very soon. This niche or purpose will be to your advantage, to your upliftment, and to your happiness. There are many things to do in your earth's sphere, you have a path to tread, and we know that you will tread it wisely and well. We have faith and trust in you, otherwise you would not have been chosen.

There are many spiritual gifts for all to receive, if you would just be aware and know they are there for you to grasp. Look within each and every day and be ready to accept these gifts of wisdom and knowledge from that Great Divine, that Great Source. And know that within your hearts are the blessings of peace and enlightenment which surpass all understanding. Allow those hearts to ring forth with enthusiasm, as the bells in your churches.

And now, my children, I give you a special blessing – may you all have an abundance of love, an abundance of serenity, and may the doves of peace fly over your heads always.

Blend the Spiritual and the Material as One

As we come together again, we entrust ourselves to the Great Divine, asking that we receive nothing but the best. We know that as we ask, so it will be revealed to us. Know well that what you desire most, what you want to happen within your little group, will materialize.

You know that when you desire certain things to happen you send out the thought which will be energized. Know full well that as you send out your thoughts, they become a reality. We ask that the laws reveal themselves to you, so that you may walk in truth and walk within those Divine Walls.

My children, you have passed through many experiences of learning in that Divine Light, the Source of all things. You have come to that awareness spiritually and materially, and we ask that this understanding be blended as one, so that you may live your life to the full, materially and spiritually.

As you know, there is no separating the two, and as you come to this awareness you will come to a spiritual condition whereby you will have developed the faculties of clairvoyance and clairaudience. You will know of things before they happen, you will know the spoken word before it is spoken. These things you will begin to experience as you blend the two, the spiritual and the material together.

This awareness will bring about the intuition that you desire. So go forth into the Divine Presence, that pure white light, which you have experienced and where you know you can have all things on a much higher level by and through your realizations and experiences in our little group.

So, my children, go forth into the garden of happiness, and live your life to the full each and every day. Add to your experiences as they are shown to you, and know that you will be well guided. Take your knowledge and use it well. Know what you desire in your life. Send out the appropriate thoughts and understand that each desire will be fulfilled.

Realizations

My children be aware of things happening to you on your material world, and when you achieve this awareness, use it wisely and well.

As you receive these realizations, both materially and spiritually, I assure you that when you reach awareness on your material world, you reach awareness on the spiritual plane as well. There are many things you can realize and become aware of, and once you do, do not cast them aside and say, "I have had a realization." You must hold it in your heart, for until you become fully aware of the realization, you will not make progress on the spiritual level.

I know, for I have seen it happen many times. I have heard many people say that they have had a wonderful realization, and then they leave it at that. They do nothing further about it. They lose the value of what they have received and what has been given to them.

When your brothers and sisters speak to you in this manner, they bring the realizations for you to grasp, be they material or spiritual. My children, examine all the words spoken to you, for they are of great value in helping you along your pathway.

May you receive the blessings of your realizations, and may you become more aware of the blessings you can acquire from your realization and awareness. You must look for them on your material world and the spiritual world. Let us be aware of all things happening around us here and now, as we join our brothers and sisters who are all happily waiting and willing to help us.

Blessed are the Peacemakers

My children, we are here for a purpose, and that purpose will be fulfilled by and through the power of the Divine Mind, that Source, that Intelligence that knows all things. Without it we would be as nothing.

As one having reached that awareness, much can be accomplished, both on your side of life and ours. There is a great harmony and a blending of souls, one with another. With that blending comes love, a Divine Love that surpasses all understanding. It is a love which nothing can take away from. We have that awareness and understanding of all these things, and now you, my children, have become aware, each and everyone.

I am going to take something which that great teacher said many years ago. It was said to his followers, to his disciples. Jesus, the Christ said, "Blessed are the peacemakers, for they shall become the children of God." Now what did Jesus mean? He did *not* mean that we had to be peacemakers by allowing some to dominate others.

No, what Jesus meant was that unless you have the peace of God in your heart and mind, you can in no way become a child of God. Therefore do not allow worries, fears and frustrations to mar that Divine Love, that Divine

Peace within each of you. When you have these worries, you cannot have the peace.

So, my children, become peacemakers in your own house, and in a short time you will become children of God. Allow no one to tell you otherwise, because it is the peace within and from the heart that makes you a child of God's.

And now, my children, I do thank you for allowing me to speak with you in this manner. Without your help I could not be here, as it is through your love that I am able to come, and it is through your being children of God that I can come. So go forward and remember, each and everyone of you have many blessings and much Divine Love. . . . "Blessed are the peacemakers for they shall be called the children of God."

Use Your Knowledge Well

Greetings, my children! Be still and know that the love of the Great White Spirit surrounds us at this moment. Know it, for that love is there for you to reach out to, here and now. May you always know the peace and the understanding within your hearts, and may you always draw from the knowledge of the well of life which is available to all.

Remember, my children, the prayers of many are with you to help and guide you, and know that each time you come together in this manner the tie and the bond of love is strengthened, as there will be no weak link in that bond. At no time will we allow any weak links to gather strength. Know and understand this!

My children, you may wonder why we strive to teach you the laws of the universe, the laws of that Great Energy or Spirit, call it what you may! As you know, when you pass over to our side of life, you bring your earthly memories. Would you have those memories be regretful because of rejection of learning, or would you rather come to our side of life and know that you can go further with your learning?

My children, this is the reason we come to those who desire knowledge and who we know will use this knowledge well. Some people fall by the wayside. As one of the masters said, "Some seeds are sown on barren ground, some grow so far and then they die." Some people fade out for a time, and unless they come to that understanding and that learning, they will have many regrets when they pass to our side of life, because they carry with them their memories. That is where one aspect of your Heaven and Hell comes in, do you understand?

It must be very frustrating to a person when he has learned and travelled the pathway so far and then he loses it and travels by another road. But each one treads his own path, as no one can tread it for him. That is the reason we come to you, to reach out and attempt to help just a little, to encourage and guide you along the pathway.

My children, you can either accept or reject, and at this point we know your choice. We have no fears for the future of anyone here. We know deeply that all will be well, as each and everyone is part of that Great Universe, that Divine Purpose. There is much knowledge in that universe. You have a mind to use, my children. Use it well and gather from the knowledge around you within the spheres of existence, knowing full well that you can have anything you desire, anything you wish. We know at this point that you will not use this enlightenment wrongly. I have told you to speak with authority. Now I say use the knowledge you have with authority, use your mind with authority and remember you can hurt no one but yourself!

My children, realize that you are on the road to progress. Progression is yours. Do not look back, look forward always, and remember that you yourself are an authority on all things. Use this knowledge, use it wisely, and all will be well.

No Dividing of Worlds

You cannot have the intellectual understanding of God's laws without the true realizations in the heart, for it would be useless. When you gain the greater understanding of those laws, it is a great realization, and as you go along your pathway weaving the pattern of your life day by day realizing the wonderful laws of creation and God, what you weave now within your material world, so you will also weave when you come to our side of life. You will live your life in the spirit world doing what you desire. Do you realize there is no great dividing between your world and our world?

The only difference is the rate of vibration in which we live. We have the same as you have on the material world. We have beautiful homes. We have beautiful flowers, the colors of which you could not begin to describe, as they are much more vibrant than those of your flowers and their perfumes are much more fragrant. We all weave our pattern working to help others, and you all are working towards the goal whereby you will be able to help many others on our side of life when the time comes for you to pass the Great Divide, which will not be for many years yet, as you all have much to learn upon the material world.

What I am saying, my children, is take those realizations and accept them. Know that once you receive them, they will give you a greater understanding of all God's laws.

We Shall Meet Again

Greetings, my children! May we draw from that Great White Brotherhood which is around and about each and everyone. May we draw from the knowledge, the understanding and the learning that we share, one with another.

If you will allow that Force, that Energy, to flow freely, then we will be working together in harmony as teachers and students of the Divine Light.

As we go forward together, ever forward into the brightness, may we always share our knowledge and understanding, one with another. As we gain that greater understanding we know that we shall always receive the best of all things.

And now, my dear children, have faith and trust in God, in that Great Divine Spirit, and with His blessings, go ever forward in love, peace and truth.

My children, we shall meet again.

A Spiritual Prayer

Oh, Great White Spirit, we come before thee silently. We ask that you would open our hearts and reveal thy truth to us in order that we may absorb the knowledge which is given to us at this time by and through your Divine Will.

We know that all knowledge is available to us inasmuch as we wish to receive it. We ask that you would light the lamp for our hearts and minds. Clear away all those undesirable thoughts so that we may have a clear channel to receive what is readily available to us.

We ask, Oh, Great White Spirit, that you would watch over each and everyone and give a special blessing to all the brothers and sisters, seen and unseen, that they may walk in your truth and in your light at all times.